Sunny B
presents

KANSAS SYMBOLS

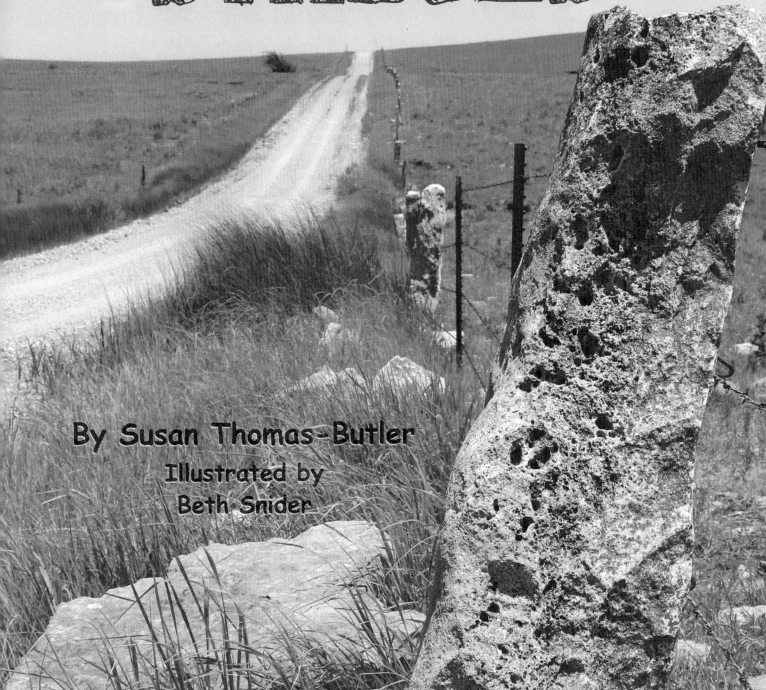

By Susan Thomas-Butler

Illustrated by
Beth Snider

Thank you to my illustrator Beth Snider for creating Sunny B, Bob Gress for donating the meadowlark picture, Brad Mangas for the Little Bluestem photograph donation, USDA-NRCS for the soil picture, my kids for their support and to my husband for the countless hours in the design of this book.

My name is Sunny B and I am a honeybee, the state insect. Come with me and I will show you the symbols of Kansas.

Kansas is in the middle of the United States.
There are about 2.8 million people living there.

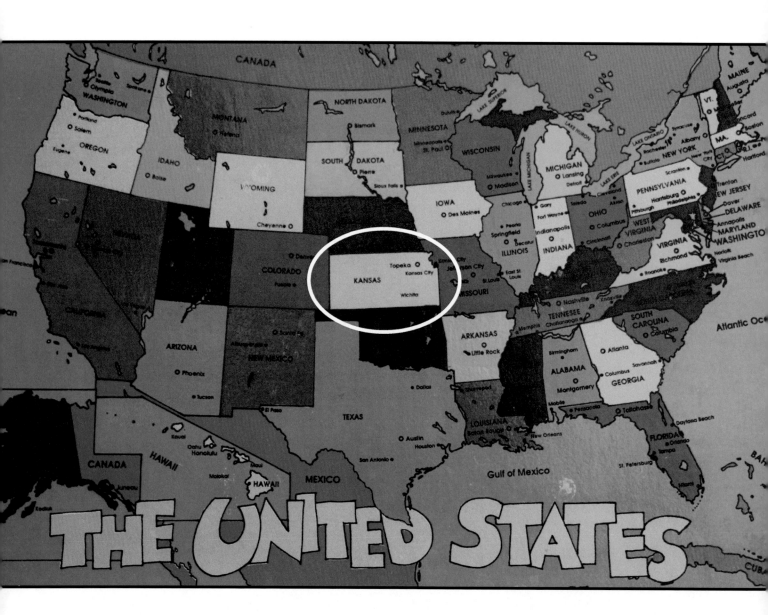

The state was named after the Kanza Indians.

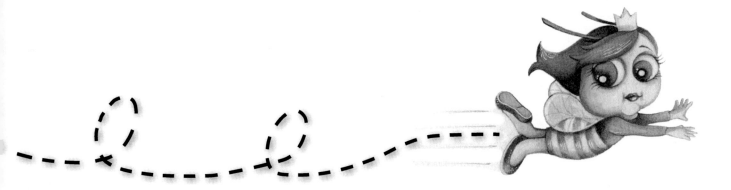

Kansas became a state on January 29, 1861.
This is known as Kansas Day.

The laws are made at the capitol in Topeka. I fly to the top of the dome while humans climb the 296 steps.

Looking down

Looking up

The seal

The State Motto is Ad Astra Per Aspera which means "to the stars through difficulty."

The flag

KANSAS

These are my friends from the beehive.
Our job is to make honey and pollinate.

What does the Queen Bee say to the worker bee when she is being bad?
Bee-Hive Yourself!

The American Bison is the state animal, but people call it the buffalo. Actually, buffaloes live in Africa and South Asia. Bison live at state parks and farms. Bison can run faster than I can fly.

American Bison

Water Buffalo

Home on the Range is the state song.

Kansas farmers grow wheat.

It can be used to make bread.

The cottonwood tree leaves are triangular and shiny. It has fluffy covered seeds.

Can you see my friend Fuzzy on this sunflower?

The sunflower is the state flower. Kansas is called "The Sunflower State."

The Western Meadowlark, the state
bird, builds a nest on the ground in
a clump of grass which makes
it hard to find.

The Kansas state reptile is the Ornate Box Turtle. It spends its life on land, not in water.

The Barred Tiger Salamander is the state amphibian. It is nocturnal, meaning it sleeps during the day and hunts at night. It makes no sound and likes to hide in the dirt.

Little Bluestem is the state grass.
It grows between two and five feet tall.

Soybeans

HARNEY

The state soil is Harney Loam Silt.
Kansas relies on it for growing crops.

Corn

What goes zzub zzub?
A bee flying backwards!

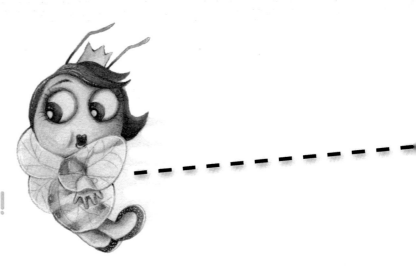

Thank you for letting me show
you my bee-autiful state!

FACTS ABOUT KANSAS

Population - 2.8 million people

Founded - January 29, 1861

Capitol - Topeka

Motto - Ad Astra Per Aspera (to the stars through difficulty)

Insect - Honeybee

Animal - American Bison

Song - Home On The Range

Tree - Cottonwood

Flower - Wild Native Sunflower

Bird - Western Meadowlark

Reptile - Ornate Box Turtle

Amphibian - Barred Tiger Salamander

Grass - Little Bluestem

Soil - Harney Loam Silt

Made in the USA
Lexington, KY
06 January 2018